Rudolf Schnackenburg

CHRIST—
PRESENT AND
COMING

Translated by Edward Quinn

Fortress Press
PHILADELPHIA

Translated by Edward Quinn from the German *Deutet die Zeichen der Zeit*, published by Verlag Herder, Freiburg, 1976, © Verlag Herder, Freiburg im Breisgau, 1976.

Translation © The Society for Promoting Christian Knowledge, London and Fortress Press, Philadelphia, 1978.

Library of Congress Cataloging in Publication Data

Schnackenburg, Rudolf, 1914—
  Christ, present and coming.

Translation of Deutet die Zeichen der Zeit.
  1. Eschatology—Meditations. I. Title.
BT823.S3613 1978   236   77-15246
ISBN 0-8006-1328-7

6504L77   Printed in the United States of America   1-1328

CONTENTS

ACKNOWLEDGEMENT

Biblical quotations from the Revised Standard Version of the Bible, copyrighted 1946, 1952, © 1971, 1973 by the Division of Christian Education of the National Council of the Churches of Christ in the USA, are used by permission.

PREFACE

These meditations, linked with texts of the New Testament, were first delivered orally in a rather different form. In Advent 1974 I was invited by the university chaplaincy to preach on the same theme in the Cathedral in Münster, Westphalia. They appear here in print as the result of further reflection. They are not meant to be more than a modest attempt to consider the pressing question of the future in the light of Jesus' message and its reception in the primitive Church.

RUDOLF SCHNACKENBURG

Jesus said to the multitudes, 'When you see a cloud rising in the west, you say at once, "A shower is coming:" and so it happens. And when you see the south wind blowing, you say, "There will be scorching heat:" and it happens. You hypocrites! You know how to interpret the appearance of earth and sky; but why do you not know how to interpret the present time?'

LUKE 12.54-6

Times of upheaval turn our thoughts to the future. Can anyone doubt that ours is such a time? The agitation and unrest which have affected the younger generation in the past decade, leading first to protest and violence and then to perplexity and acquiescence, are connected to no small degree with the question of the future. Alvin Toffler has spoken of the 'future shock' which has come upon the people of our time. In the book of that title (The Bodley Head 1970) he provides detailed evidence of the vast changes which have taken place in a few decades, leaving far behind the developments of centuries. It is as if modern man had made a mighty leap forward, but is mentally incapable of coping with it.

Anxiety about the future

The American anthropologist, Margaret Mead, observes in her work, *Culture and Commitment. A Study of the Generation Gap* (The Bodley Head 1970), that the present generation is gripped by completely new awareness of life. Its members see themselves as immigrants into a new country. Concern for the future is the deeper reason for their revolutionary protest against existing institutions and systems. They want to break out of the constraints of the efficiency-oriented and consumer society. They are on the defensive against the total management and planning of man, against the pointlessness of what seems to be an irreversible development. Meanwhile a change has come about. Not a few young people are turning away from extremist attempts, perceiving the stupidity of violence and trying by reflection and meditation to gain inward strength, in order to continue on their way in all the unrest and insecurity. The rapid succession and simultaneity of contrary attitudes and trends is confusing, and no one can tell which forces will prevail or what direction the journey into the future is taking.

Christian faith too is drawn into the unrest and upheaval of our time. For it is held by people who are caught and shaken, like all the others, by the storms of their time. But if it is true that doubt about the future is a hidden, powerful cause of unrest and insecurity, then we may also look to our faith for an answer; for Christianity is a religion of hope. Can this hope persist in face of the darkness, the needs and anxieties of our time? Can the message of Jesus give us some gleams of hope for the future, provide interpretations of our historical situation, offer directives for the way we have to go and for our behaviour in society?

The season of Advent particularly invites us to this kind of reflection. Advent means arrival, the arrival of the Lord. In the liturgy in a singular conspectus the threefold arrival of Christ is perceptible: one which has already occurred, the historical coming of Jesus, fulfilling the expectation of former times and the predictions of the prophets; then a coming of Jesus at the end of time, one which is still awaited; finally a coming at the present time, a spiritual coming by grace which provides a reason and a stimulus for our expectation. In meditative reflection, in the eucharistic encounter, in the congregational celebration, we have a continually new experience of the tension between fulfilment and expectation. What the liturgical texts express with extreme conciseness are aspects of our faith which enable us to experience the mystery of our time and the challenge of history. It is against this background that we must consider how we are to cope with our times and the future which is coming upon us.

The present time calls us away from our quiescence and self-assurance. The futurologists tell us that our present-day society cannot continue indefinitely in face of the accelerated population-growth, the exhaustion of energy sources, the destruction of the environment, the unjust distribution of essential goods, the insane competition in armaments. The limits of growth can be foreseen. Economic crises and armed conflicts, natural disasters and famines affect mankind on a global scale. Poverty and distress in underdeveloped countries are swelling into a current carrying everything with it. In the rich nations new acts of violence are breaking out and there is no end to the armaments race. The outlook for the future seems dark and gloomy.

Answers from the message of Jesus

Is there anything in Jesus' message which could help us in this situation? Can primitive Christianity, which took up his message and carried it into the world of that time, provide answers? If we consider the present world-situation not merely superficially, but seek out the reasons which lie deeper and observe people's behaviour, then Jesus' message and its many echoes in the primitive Christian communities even acquire an outstanding importance for our time and for our way into the future. For man with his attitudes and decisions is still the most important and the least certain factor entering into calculations of the future, even into the prognoses of realistic futurologists. Although Jesus turns to his contemporaries in order to equip them for what is coming, his message contains statements, appeals, and demands which concern everyone, including the people of our technical age. His words, related to concrete situations, have a permanent force and continually gain new relevance in new historical circumstances. The primitive Church understood this when it applied Jesus' words to its own situation and on each occasion differently in the light of the circumstances of the different communities. Its teachers and theologians penetrated the message of Jesus with the light of faith, and acquired a new understanding of human history and Christian life in this world. Even in primitive Christianity there were various forms of Christian behaviour in the world. Not that we could simply adopt these attitudes; but they stimulate our thinking and prompt our will, to enable us better to cope with our time and our future. The words of Jesus, carefully collected, put together, and interpreted for that time in the Gospels, are primordial words inexhaustible in their meaning and continually fertile.

'Signs of the time'

Jesus spoke of the signs of the time. He was not making an analysis of world-conditions at the time and prospects of the future, nor a prognosis in the light of human foresight. His words were addressed to men against the background of historical experience and were meant to lead to reflection and to a change in their behaviour. They amount to a prophetic call behind which is the message which Jesus wants to deliver in God's name. When and on what occasion Jesus spoke these words can no longer be decided. As we shall see, Luke fits them into a context which he has himself created. He emphasizes the fact that they are directed to the 'multitudes', in order to make it clear that they concern all men. But the charge made in the middle of the speech—'you hypocrites'—introduces a polemical note and provides a reason to assume that on Jesus' lips the speech was originally addressed to people who had closed their hearts to his message. The same invective is found shortly afterwards (13.15) in Jesus' answer to the leader of the synagogue who was scandalized by Jesus' cure on the sabbath. For Jesus 'hypocrites' are people who oppose God's intentions out of narrow-mindedness and evil will, who will not admit what God evidently does for men and do not draw any conclusions for their own action. The expression therefore does not refer merely to people who dissemble and conceal their true thoughts: hypocrites are those who resist the known truth, who oppose God.

Although Jesus' speech therefore applies originally to his obstinate opponents, it is still appropriate for Luke to turn it into an appeal to all men. For are we not all in danger of overlooking, of not wanting to see, the signs of the times, since they call us away from bourgeois comfort, indifference, and inactivity? The frequent exhortations to vigilance and preparedness found in the preaching of Jesus were applied by the primitive Church to the specific situation of its members. Luke sees especially the temptation of riches and prosperity: 'As for what fell among the thorns, they are those who hear, but as they go on their way they are choked by the cares and riches and pleasures of life' (8.14). 'Take heed to yourselves lest your hearts be weighed down with dissipation and drunkenness and cares of this life, and that day come upon you suddenly like a snare' (21.34).

Knowing God's hidden working

But what are the signs of the time which Jesus has in mind? Are they signs of menace or of salvation? The weather-signs, which are all the indication given in the

11

text, are phenomena to be observed every day, to which the countryman especially looks. They do not permit us to look either for disaster or for a favourable turn of events. The first sign mentioned, indicating rain, is something welcome and desirable in Palestinian conditions. In the books of the Kings we read that, after a terrible drought which lasted three years and led to a severe famine, God announced to the prophet Elijah the coming of the long-desired rain. The prophet climbed up to the top of Carmel, crouched to the ground, and put his head between his knees. Then he ordered his servant to go up and look out to the sea. The servant went up, looked out, and reported that there was nothing to see. Again and again the prophet sent his servant up. At the seventh time the servant reported that a cloud, no larger than a man's hand, was rising out of the sea. It was not long before the skies were darkened by storm and clouds and a heavy rain began (1 Kings 18.42-5). So too the 'cloud rising in the west', of which Jesus spoke, could be understood as a token bringing happiness. But the heat-bringing south wind, mentioned after this, is feared because of the way it scorches everything; like the east wind from the desert, it dries up springs and fountains (Hos. 13.15).

So the signs of the weather cited by Jesus are meant on the whole to illustrate merely a turning point which is to be expected. In one of the parallel texts of Matthew, not however attested by the oldest manuscripts, other examples are chosen: 'When it is evening, you say, "It will be fair weather; for the sky is red." And in the morning, "It will be stormy today, for the sky is red and threatening" ' (16.2-3). Here a very similar outward sign—red sky at evening and morning—leads to different prognoses in different circumstances and thus illustrates man's capacity to judge everything very precisely, without knowing how to interpret the 'signs of the times'. The examples from meteorology then are merely metaphors and analogies with which Jesus gives expression to his concern: men lack the readiness to see the signals given by Jesus of a more deeply significant happening, a turning point already becoming apparent, and to draw from all this conclusions for themselves.

A similar image is available in the parable of the fig tree which is brought into the great speech about the future: 'Look at the fig tree, and all the trees; as soon as they come out in leaf, you see for yourselves and know that the summer is already near.' In this case Luke expresses more clearly what the expected happening is, for he continues: 'So also, when you see these things taking place, you know that the kingdom of God is near' (21.29-31). This parable too now acquires a special meaning within the context of the 'eschatological discourse', a meaning which leads us to think of the signs of the Son of man and of God's kingdom in its perfection. Only Luke mentions the kingdom of God here; it is however predominant at the centre of Jesus' preaching. As a result of his widespread activity among the people, the parable itself on Jesus' lips will have drawn attention to the already visible signs that God's rule is imminent; not, as in the end-time address for the later Church, to signs of Jesus' coming at the end. Thus the parables of the weather-signs and of the fig tree becoming green complement one another. Jesus is sure that things are happening in his time which make God's activity certain for eyes that see and hearts prepared for it. What else does God's rule and kingdom mean? For God does not rule like an earthly despot with the visible machinery of power, but in a hidden way, in signs, and yet effectively and perceptibly. There is another saying from the oldest Jesus-tradition which is addressed to the disciples: 'Blessed are the eyes which see what you see! For I tell you that many prophets and kings desired to see what you see, and did not see it, and to hear what you hear, and did not hear it' (Luke 10.23-4).

Hence from a variety of individual sayings attributed to Jesus a basic chord of his proclamation emerges: God is active in bringing about a turn of events. The signs of his activity are already perceptible. They are happening in the sight of men—in Jesus' appearing on the scene, in his preaching and in the deeds accompanying this, in a hopeful transformation of the conditions in which men are placed. Not however that anything sensational is implied in this, no turn for the better at one stroke, no final banishment of all misery, of all suffering. There will be no 'heavenly intervention' in events on earth, to break the power of evil without men's co-operation, to change the political and economic conditions, to create a new order of things.

'Signs from heaven'?

Jesus drew attention to the signs given by God for our time, but repeatedly refused to perform a 'sign from heaven'. When he was challenged to do so, he said: 'This generation is an evil generation; it seeks a sign but no sign shall be given to it except the sign of Jonah. For as Jonah became a sign to the men of Nineveh, so will the Son of man be to this generation' (Luke 11.29-30). It is unbelief which leads people mistakenly to demand a striking sign, even though the signs of God's activity are clearly to be seen. It is a result of misunderstanding Jesus' preaching that they expect from him extraordinary miracles, spectacular events, when he wants only to tell them of the miracle of God's love and to make them aware of their own ability to love, to be converted at heart. In this sense he is himself the sign of God for men and it was in this way that the primitive Church interpreted the sign of Jonah.

It is similar in John's Gospel. Jesus showed the

generous love of God by providing abundant food for the multitude; but afterwards some Jews pressed him: 'What sign do you do, that we may see, and believe you? What work do you perform? Our fathers ate the manna in the wilderness; as it is written, "He gave them bread from heaven to eat" ' (John 6.30-1). Again the evangelist interprets it rightly with the understanding of faith when he makes Jesus answer: 'I am the bread of life; he who comes to me shall not hunger, and he who believes in me shall never thirst.' But to those Jews he retorted: 'You have seen me and yet do not believe' (6.35-6).

Call to repent

From time to time Jesus seems to have fastened on to external events in which he recognized a call of God. There is a tradition peculiar to Luke, referring to an occasion when people came to Jesus and told him of the Galileans whom Pilate had executed at the time of sacrifice, so that their blood was mingled with that of the sacrificial animals. He then asked if they thought that these Galileans were great sinners, since this had happened to them, while other Galileans were not. On the contrary, he claimed, they too would perish in the same way if they did not repent. He took the opportunity to remind them also of the eighteen who had been killed by a falling tower in Jerusalem. Were they guilty of greater sins than all the others in Jerusalem? On the contrary, if they would not repent, they too would suffer the same fate (Luke 13.1-5).

For Jesus, God also speaks through temporal events. He does not attribute these directly to God, but in fact rejects the popular opinion that the people to whom something evil has happened were punished by God as particularly great sinners. But to people upset by these things he gives cause for reflection and exhorts them—as the old prophets frequently did—to see in the events a call to repentance. Since Luke relates these things shortly after the words about the weather-signs, for him they will be among the signs of the times which Jesus had in mind. But again this is the view of the evangelist which he expresses by combining his traditions. We can scarcely conclude from all this that Jesus was thinking mainly of menaces when he referred to the weather-signs. We saw that the first of the examples drawn from observing the weather is a sign promising blessing. Jesus was not primarily a preacher of penance and judgement, like some Old Testament prophets and also John the Baptist, but 'God's herald of joy', proclaiming mercy and salvation. His threat of judgement is only the reverse side for those who will not accept his good tidings.

Being open to what is new

According to Luke Jesus never speaks in so many words of signs which his hearers ought to observe, but says—literally translated—'Why then do you not test this time?' (12.56). In this respect the word translated as 'time' is not one that refers to chronological succession, but to the right time, favourable to action, calling for decision. It has entered into our usage as a foreign word. It is the *kairos*, the opportune time, containing in itself something important, a time that is granted and not to be missed. By 'this time' Jesus means the present, in which God's mercy—and of course his demanding will—is proclaimed. Although Jesus does not directly name himself as the one who brings all this about—he makes his person secondary to his mission and his work—it cannot be doubted that he is thinking of everything that is happening through him. The cures and the expulsion of demons which he accomplishes are signs of God's salvific will. His table-fellowship with tax-collectors and sinners (Luke 5.27-32) demonstrates God's acceptance of sinners. The words of forgiveness for the woman despised as a sinner (Luke 7.36-50) show that God wants to bestow his love on all, but that he also expects from everyone a large measure of love. It is the 'acceptable year of the Lord', as we read in the programmatic address of Jesus in Nazareth (Luke 4.19), the 'today' when the prophetic promises are fulfilled.

Seen outwardly, Jesus' time was no less full of unrest, struggle, and revolt than other times. As they had been from time immemorial, men were driven by envy and hatred, conceit, and lust for power. But with his message, behaviour, and action Jesus puts forward something new: things may not and will not continue in this way. God's increasingly visible mercy for misguided and sinful men provides the opening for a new age and is at the same time an appeal to men to lay themselves open to this new reality and themselves to become different. This also is the meaning of conversion. Believe in God's message of salvation and let yourselves be transformed by God's love for all men! (cf. Mark 1.15.). Only where the will to repent is lacking will Jesus' call become a warning, his word a judgement: 'Truly, I say to you, the tax collectors and the harlots go into the kingdom of God before you' (Matt. 21.31).

Is Jesus' message utopian?

Once we understand this intention of Jesus, we of the twentieth century may begin to feel some doubt: Did Jesus not deceive himself with his optimism? In the centuries which have passed since his time, in the 'Christian' centuries, have men changed? Has God's blessed rule, proclaimed by Jesus, become effective and perceptible even merely in parts of society, even merely in interpersonal relationships? Have people allowed themselves to be conquered and visibly changed by God's mercy and love? Are the really visible signs of our time not pointing to storm and imminent disaster?

Before attempting an answer, it is a good thing to be quite clear about something else. For the primitive Church, which recorded and handed on the message of Jesus, this problem was in principle already as urgent as it is for ourselves. Had not Jesus failed with his message and his appeal among his own contemporaries, in the people of Israel? Had not this herald of the love of God, this benefactor of men (cf. Acts 10.38), this innocent-righteous man, even been charged with rebellion, delivered up to the Romans, and brought like a common criminal to the cross?

The primitive Church was also aware that Jesus had announced an *early* turning point, the *imminent* dawn of the kingdom of God, and it continued to be actively occupied with the 'immediate expectation'. Nevertheless, it had not mistaken the meaning of Jesus' words. It was true that his resurrection had opened up a wholly new prospect and roused a hope going beyond all the darkness of the present world, beyond the enigmatic course of history. But the early Christians continued to live in this world and wanted to take Jesus' words as directives for their earthly life and for their behaviour in human society. In this respect it is the evangelist Luke in particular, a cultured hellenist, who not only conveyed the message of Jesus historically to the communities, but also interpreted it for their own time. For him Jesus' words, directly addressed to his contempories in relation to particular situations, lose nothing of their force and relevance for the Christian readers to whom he turns one or two generations later. For him also there are signs of the times, signs of his time, which continue to provoke Jesus' exhortation: 'Test this time!'

Continuing steadfastly in faith

In all this it is possible to observe that Luke has shifted the emphasis to disastrous manifestations and threatening signs. In the context of our passage he has combined those traditional sayings of Jesus which imply an externally depressing outlook. First of all there are the words of warning to the disciples: 'Do you think that I have come to give peace on earth? No, I tell you, but rather division; for henceforth in one house there will be five divided, three against two and two against three; they will be divided, father against son and son against father, mother against daughter and daughter against her mother, mother-in-law against her daughter-in-law and daughter-in-law against her mother-in-law' (12.51-3). These pictures are similar to those painted in Jewish apocalypses (extra-biblical writings outlining the future) of a future time of distress. The text is meant to draw attention to coming trials and temptations of the disciples, to conflict on account of faith which will divide families. To this Luke has added Jesus' words about the signs of the time and addressed them to the multitudes.

Then there follows a further parable, describing a critical situation: 'As you go with your accuser before the magistrate, make an effort to settle with him on the way, lest he drag you to the judge, and the judge hand you over to the officer, and the officer put you in prison' (12.58). Here too we find the threat of judgement and the urgent warning to reflect and repent. Thus the text is appropriately linked to the other—already mentioned—about the Galileans whose blood was mingled with that of the sacrificed animals and about the people killed by the falling tower.

It is clear that Luke is concerned mainly with the exhortation to repent. The signs of the time are pressing; the Christian must take a decisive stand, detach himself from earthly entanglements. Luke has by no means over-looked or forgotten Jesus' message of salvation; but he promises real salvation only at the *parousia*, the second coming of Christ. As Jesus himself 'must suffer many things and be rejected by this generation' (Luke 17.25), so we also must 'continue in the faith, and . . . through many tribulations . . . enter the kingdom of God' (Acts 14.22). This is Luke's outlook for his time and his communities.

The persistent claim

Has the evangelist thus misrepresented the message or the intention of Jesus? No. What he has done is to apply Jesus' words to the situation of the Church in the eighties of the first century and attempted to put before his readers Jesus' permanent demand as it concerns them. He conceals nothing of what Jesus proclaimed as his gospel. It is Luke in particular who has preserved for us some of the most precious elements of Jesus' preaching: the parables of the lost sheep, the lost coin, the prodigal son (chapter 15). They form—so to speak—the heart of his book and have rightly been described as 'the gospel within the gospel'. We have this evangelist also to thank for the parable of the good Samaritan (10.30-7), the story of the woman who was a great sinner (7.36-50) and of Zacchaeus, the chief tax-collector (19.1-10), and a number of other details. But he also wanted to draw the conclusions for his time and for his Christians in regard to Christian behaviour in the world and to bring home to later believers the continuing claim of Jesus' preaching.

The primitive Church as a whole proceeded in a way similar to that of Luke. For it Jesus Christ was God's Yes to the promises (2 Cor. 1.20), God's final word to mankind (Heb. 1.2). For that reason the words of the earthly Jesus became the words of the still living Christ, with ever new impulses for the present time. In a homily on Psalm 95 the author of the letter to the Hebrews cries to his readers: 'Therefore, as the Holy Spirit says, "To-day, when you hear his voice, do not harden your hearts" . . . exhort one another every day, as long as it is called "today" ' (Heb. 3.7-8, 13). Paul quotes a saying of Isaiah, 'At the acceptable time I have listened to you, and helped you on the day of salvation', and continues: 'Behold, now is the acceptable time; behold, now is the day of salvation' (2 Cor. 6.2). This still-enduring here and now presses us also to interpret in Jesus' sense the signs of our time.

A promise which calls for action

Like the modern futurologists, the Christian too can attempt a realistic analysis of the phenomena of the time. Like them, he can observe and test these good and bad 'weather-signs' to see what prognoses emerge. At the same time he will guard against all illusions, even those which futurologists sometimes repeat to him: that God will see that everything goes on as before and that mankind will not be involved in catastrophe. The Christian can and must approve the determination to utilize all the achievements of science and technology, to seize all possibilities of planning and making provision, to improve economic and social structures, to carry out a policy of prudence. For he knows that God does not directly intervene in earthly conditions and does not arbitrarily and miraculously change the course of history.

And yet the Christian will not be content with this superficial consideration. For him there are deeper reasons for world-events and other signs in our time, which are apparent only in the light of faith. It is here that the power of evil is manifested, which can bring to nothing even the best intentions and greatest efforts of the good. It is a sinister phenomenon, to which the planners of the future like to close their eyes and which nevertheless calls for constant watchfulness. But the Christian is also aware of the forces of good which flowed into the world through Jesus: that movement of redeeming love, starting out from Jesus, which continually seizes man afresh and enables him to perform actions which have no less influence on the way to the future. The Christian does not venture to work out from all this any earthly-historical prognoses of the future; but he experiences there the call of Christ to test the *kairos*, to find out what it demands from him.

It is still the time of Christ, with the promise that God God's kingdom is approaching. This hope persists, however dark the future appears. It is a hope that does not let us sleep, but calls to action—and in fact to an action and behaviour in the world which is sustained by indestructible hope.

2   DOUBTS ABOUT THE FUTURE?
THE MESSAGE OF JESUS

Being asked by the Pharisees when the kingdom of God was coming, he answered them, 'The kingdom of God is not coming with signs to be observed, nor will they say, "Lo, here it is!" or "There!" for behold, the kingdom of God is in the midst of you.'

LUKE 17.20-1

Indestructible hope? What is there to sustain such hope? Doubt about the future cannot so easily be silenced. Today it is stronger than ever. In his famous manifesto 'A Free Man's Worship' Bertrand Russell wrote: 'Brief and powerless is Man's life; on him and all his race the slow, sure doom falls pitiless and dark. Blind to good and evil, reckless of destruction, omnipotent matter rolls on its relentless way' (*The Basic Writings of Bertrand Russell 1903-1959*, Allen & Unwin 1961, p. 72).

This is the consistent view of a materialistic view of the world. 'Omnipotent matter' is the modern myth to which people have succumbed who no longer find any meaning in world-history: a variation of the ancient belief in fate which filled with gloom and depression many people of late antiquity and the declining hellenistic civilization. It is a view which is in fact opposed by modern futurologists. John Wren-Lewis writes: 'True natural science knows nothing about "omnipotent matter" . . . Omnipotent matter is like the omnipotent God of traditional religion, merely a figment of the imagination to which people have recourse in order to evade the challenge to take themselves seriously as creative beings.'

The solution suggested here is to be found therefore in man's creativity. Man is seen as a being endowed with unsuspected powers and still unexhausted abilities, who can cope with the difficulties accumulating for mankind as a result of the explosive population growth on the one hand and the increasing exhaustion of material reserves on the other. In itself this awareness of the mind which rules over matter is welcome, and it is absolutely right to appeal for the utilization of man's potential for creative imagination, for research and inventiveness, for calculating and planning.

But does all this really dispel doubts about the future? Are there not situations in which man, with all his mental power, cannot go further and must submit helplessly to the pressure of facts? Are there not obstacles within himself and resistance from outside which bring home to him the limitations of his nature? The creativity of man is circumscribed by his creatureliness. The optimists of the future, however, do not want to hear anything of this, since they suspect that behind it there is once more the flight to 'almighty God' who is expected to rescue us from all our troubles. But this is a very inadequate idea of God. God, the Creator, has granted man mind and creativity and wants him to make use of these; man however is not God, but remains a creature.

God's rule and kingdom

Jesus based on God the hope which his preaching roused in his hearers; there is no doubt about this. It is proved by the very idea which becomes the principal content of his message: rule or kingdom of God. For most people of course this once very meaningful word has become unintelligible, an empty shell of a word, with which nothing can be done. For the people of that time the

very sound of this word would revive an abundance of
ideas already available in the faith in the God of the
fathers and prophets and pointing to the future. Jesus
takes this for granted with his Jewish hearers. Nowhere
is it suggested that he explained to them what is meant
by 'kingdom of God' or that he developed the content
of its meaning. They could understand what he was
telling them when he spoke of the coming of the kingdom of God, even though it roused different expectations in them. But before we turn to this particular
message, we must perhaps go back still further and consider briefly how Jesus drew the idea from the religious
tradition of his people.

God's mandate to man

For Israel, God is the creator of heaven and earth and
also of man, who in the biblical view is the centre and
crown of creation. In the earliest creation account,
which now comes in the second place in the book of
Genesis, we read in the context of the paradise narrative: 'Then the Lord God formed man of dust from the
ground, and breathed into his nostrils the breath of life;
and man became a living being' (2.7). Today the Bible is
described as a book of 'narrative theology', because its
theology is expressed in narrative form. The ancient
('Yahwistic') account, by telling the story of man's
origin simply and vividly, tells us something about man's
nature. Man is an earthly being, as is indicated in the
play upon words in the Hebrew (adam = man, from
adamah = ground or soil), by his body closely linked to
earth and yet by his mind filled with a life which raises
him above the rest of creation and brings him close to
God. Within the paradisiac creation man takes a central
position and he is given a mandate to control it. The
ruling position, which enables him to bring the rest of
creation into his service, is illustrated by a further

25

symbolic act: the naming of all living things (2.19). In the other creation account, now in the first place, the six-day work of the priestly writing, man is created by God as the last and supreme creature on earth and appointed to rule over the earth. In Psalm 8 (the creation psalm) we read:

What is man that thou art mindful of him,
and the son of man that thou dost care for him?
Yet thou hast made him little less than God,
and dost crown him with glory and honor.
Thou hast given him dominion over the works of
    thy hands;
thou hast put all things under his feet.

Man's ability to make use of his intellectual powers in order to bring the material world into his service is also recognized as part of creation. More than that, it is a mandate from God. God conveyed to man something of his creative power ('creativity') and gave him a mandate over the world which he has never revoked. Nor did Jesus, in whose discourses and parables it is assumed that the world is God's creation, by any means want his message of the kingdom of God to deprive that mandate of its force. 'God's rule' is not a substitute for man's effort to subject the world in an earthly and historical sense to himself and to make it his world. When Jesus says his Yes to God the Creator, he is not opposed to investigation and progress on the part of mankind; he is not opposed to the development of life or to joy in the beauty of this world. He sees however, not merely this brighter side of the earthly reality, but also the dark and enigmatic aspects which burden mankind.

God's hidden activity

Mankind has behind it a history full of bitter and depressing experiences in which every nation and every human being is included and involved. The small nation of Israel acquired at an early stage a historical awareness which was linked with its religious faith. One of its primordial experiences, in which is rooted its faith in Yahweh, the God of the fathers, is the oppression in the 'house of bondage' in Egypt and the welcome liberation, which it does not ascribe to its own powers. 'The Lord brought us out of Egypt with a mighty hand and an outstretched arm, with great terror, with signs and wonders; and he brought us into this place and gave us this land, a land flowing with milk and honey' (Deut. 26.8-9). This primordial experience is continually confirmed in new historical experiences: tribulation and suffering, oppression and tyranny, failure and sin; then again rising, rescue and a new beginning, ways opening to a better future. The nation often experiences its misery and its powerlessness, all the uncertainty and fragility of human nature. But as long as it trusts in Yahweh, its God, and keeps faith with him, it does not perish.

The whole complicated history acquires a meaning only when we recognize in it the hidden guidance of God. From this religious standpoint history is continually freshly interpreted in Israel, but always with the persistent idea that God in his wisdom and power can turn to good the evil which men cause. For this he does not need to intervene directly and suddenly in the course of history: he can stir the thoughts and hearts of men as he moved the Persian King Cyrus to let the Israelites return from captivity in Babylon. He can choose men and nations in order to use them as his instruments. Faith sees God as effective in both creation and history. God is directing everything in a hidden way without depriving men of their freedom of action. But he often directs the course of history differently from what people expect. This faith was alive in Israel at the time of Jesus, as can be seen in the Magnificat, in Mary's hymn of praise (Luke 1.51-3):

He has shown strength with his arm,
he has scattered the proud in the imagination of
    their hearts,
he has put down the mighty from their thrones,
and exalted those of low degree;
he has filled the hungry with good things,
and the rich he has sent empty away.

This faith in God, who directs and guides everything
in secret, who eludes men's thoughts and opposes the
prudent and powerful, is also for Jesus the basis of his
message of salvation. In a prayer of thanksgiving, which
Jesus according to early tradition uttered at the peak of
his activity, we read: 'I thank thee, Father, Lord of
heaven and earth, that thou hast hidden these things
from the wise and understanding and revealed them to
babes; yea, Father, for such was thy gracious will' (Luke
10.21). In this 'exultant cry', as the prayer has been
called, we can see more closely into the mind of Jesus—
who was otherwise austere and reserved in regard to his
own person—and to surmise something of the mystery
by which he lived. He was aware of being deeply united
with God, whom he called his father in a special sense.
It was from his immediate relationship to God that he
gained the unshakeable certainty of his message. God,
the 'Lord of heaven and earth', is also the one who is
active at present, revealing himself in Jesus' work, but
manifesting himself only to people who do not watch
Jesus' behaviour with intellectual pride and human
arrogance, but accept his message with childlike open-
ness and readiness to believe.

This again is not a rejection of human research and
effort in fields accessible to the questing mind, but a
warning against wanting to know everything and to judge
everything about what happens on earth and makes up
the meaning of history. The very thing which is more
deeply significant, which occurs in Jesus' preaching and

actions and has a definite meaning for men and the future of mankind, is concealed under the expression 'these things': these are what Jesus sees as the essence of his message.

The meaning of the message of Jesus

What then does the message of the imminent kingdom of God imply? Jesus here refers to the consoling preaching and the blessings promised by great prophets to Israel at times of deep humiliation and powerlessness. Jesus seems to have taken up particularly the prophecy in the second part of the book of Isaiah, addressed to the exiles in Babylon. This prophet (Deutero-Isaiah) proclaims to the stricken people—so to speak—a second exodus, a new liberation like the first out of slavery in Egypt. God himself comes to redeem his people. For this the prophet uses a metaphor which vividly describes the return of the exiles under God's leadership.

A voice cries: 'In the wilderness prepare the way of
    the Lord,
make straight in the desert a highway for our God.
Every valley shall be lifted up,
    and every mountain and hill be made low;
the uneven ground shall become level,
    and the rough places a plain' (Isa. 40.3-4).

A broad and straight royal road is built, so that God can go before the repatriates. Then a herald of joy runs ahead to bring the glad tidings to Jerusalem.

How beautiful upon the mountains
    are the feet of him who brings good tidings,
who publishes peace, who brings good tidings of good,
who publishes salvation,
who says to Zion, 'Your God reigns.' (Isa. 52.7).

At this point we hear the word that has become a

standard term for us, 'good tidings' or *euangelion* (gospel), and we understand why we do not speak of Jesus' doctrine or programme, but of his message. It is a message which he brings from God and which announces something new, something that brings happiness: the kingship of God. God will finally take up his rule, which means liberation, peace, and true happiness for men. The vision of the prophet too is only a metaphor and the saying about the kingdom of God merely one form of expression drawn from the world of experience of that time in order to bring out the idea that God will bring about a new turn of events, break the power of evil, and lead men to a happy future. Here Israel's idea of God becomes effective.

> Have you not known? Have you not heard?
> The Lord is the everlasting God,
> the Creator of the ends of the earth.
> He does not faint or grow weary,
> his understanding is unsearchable (Isa. 40.28).

As God keeps faith with his creation, so too with his covenant-people and with the whole human race.

> Can a woman forget her suckling child,
> that she should have no compassion on the son of
>   her womb?
> Even these may forget,
> yet I will not forget you (Isa. 49.15).

Jesus knows that he is the herald of joy bringing to Israel the good news of God's mercy. It is striking that the parts which recapitulate and interpret Jesus' mission combine texts from the second and third parts of the book of Isaiah. Even if in this presentation they go back only to the early community or to one of the evangelists, there can be no doubt that they aptly describe Jesus' attitude. For the reader they are brought together in a concentrated form in particular situations and recapitulate what shines out from the whole activity of Jesus. Luke wants to make this clear at the very beginning of Jesus' entry on the scene, in his home-town of Nazareth, although the other Gospels place this appearance at a later stage. On a Sabbath at the synagogue in Nazareth Jesus has the scroll brought to him and reads from the book of Isaiah:

> The Spirit of the Lord is upon me,
> because he has anointed me to preach good news to
>   the poor.
> He has sent me to proclaim release to the captives
> and recovering of sight to the blind,
> to set at liberty those who are oppressed,
> to proclaim the acceptable year of the Lord (Luke
>   4.18-19).

From the ancient sayings-source, used by Matthew and Luke, comes the answer to John the Baptist, that he is to be told what his messengers have seen and heard:

> The blind receive their sight, the lame walk, lepers
>   are cleansed, and the deaf hear,
> the dead are raised up, the poor have good news
>   preached to them.
> And blessed is he who takes no offence at me (Luke
>   7.22-3).

It now becomes still more clear why Jesus' cures and other salvific actions are regarded as signs of the time he has brought about: in them is realized something of what those prophets promised for the coming time when God is to rule as king. It is also clear that it is not a question of individual actions, but of all Jesus' activity; for the preaching of salvation to the poor is particularly stressed. There are sufficient traces of the fact that Jesus saw his preaching and his actions in this light. Through him God wills to fulfil his salvific intentions; he says, for example: 'If it is by the finger of God that

I cast out demons, then the kingdom of God has come upon you' (Luke 11.20).

The dawn of God's rule in Jesus

Thus in Jesus' activity the rule of God already dawns, an inwardly liberating rule, since its law is not domination but service. The multitudes flock towards him, among them many who are only looking for material help, but not a few also who have been thrilled and touched by his preaching. They want to have part in the kingdom of God of which he speaks; they understand too that this includes demands on themselves. Jesus flatters no one: anyone who wants to enter more closely into the following of Jesus must be resolved to abandon his possessions, perhaps even his family. Jesus is not a demagogue, seeking to sweep people off their feet with fine words and enticing promises, to draw them into a revolutionary campaign, as others did at that time. He wants to gather people together by a call of God's love and to rouse them to the utmost love. What he proclaims is the beginning of the rule of God.

Nevertheless, the actual, perfected rule of God remains a promise. Jesus teaches his disciples to pray: 'Your kingdom come.' In many parables he chooses metaphors for the future kingdom of God which are intelligible to his contemporaries: festival, marriage, joyous banquet, harvest, promised land, kingdom of peace. In his prophetic, insistent manner Jesus offers a prospect of the kingdom of God as immediately at hand: 'The kingdom of God is at hand' (Mark 1.15). In his preaching of the kingdom of God there is a tension between fulfilment and promise and it is just this expectation, oriented to the end, which presses for a decision: 'No one who puts his hand to the plow and looks back is fit for the kingdom of God' (Luke 9.62).

But in the popular, organized movement called forth by Jesus a phase seems to have occurred when the first waves of enthusiasm died down. The leading groups in Jewry remained aloof and sceptical. Jesus did nothing to win over the scribes; on the contrary, he proclaimed with unparalleled freedom God's will as something of which he was certain. He criticized the many petty regulations which these guardians of the law had set up —certainly with good intentions—to protect the holy law and to organize all life in accordance with its terms. But this led to narrow human interpretation and to servitude and internal depression, as well as to arrogance, self-satisfaction, and pride on the part of the legally devout. Jesus saw through human narrow-mindedness and was indignant when those who could not satisfy the stiff requirements of the law were despised by the others. His ideas were quite different, as he makes clear in the parable of the Pharisee and the tax-collector. The Pharisee stands up in the temple before God and boasts: 'God, I thank thee that I am not like other men, extortioners, unjust, adulterers, or even like this tax collector' (Luke 18.11); he finds no favour in God's sight. But the tax-collector remains standing behind and prays sincerely: 'God be merciful to me a sinner' (Luke 18.13); he obtains God's mercy and returns home justified. Such attacks made these respectable people suspicious of Jesus, and their disapproval and hostility quietly increased. Being influential among the ordinary people, they were able to sow the seeds of distrust and doubt.

We cannot now follow the ebb and flow of public opinion in the light of the individual stories related in the Gospels. But one thing is certain: disappointment and doubt increased, with the result that a number of Jesus' supporters turned away from him.

Jesus was not on the wrong track with his message.

It is true that we do not know on what occasions he related these 'parables of growth' which are now combined in a single chapter; but they seem to be connected with rising doubts. Mark narrates three such parables: those of the sower, of the growing seed, and of the mustard seed (Mark 4). What is common to all these is that there is always an initial stage (sowing) and an end-stage (harvest, abundance). The sower sows his seed in hope, but a great deal is lost. Some seeds fall on the path and the birds come and devour them. Others fall on stony ground; they shoot up, but the rising sun scorches the young plants, since they have no deep roots. Others again fall among thorns and the thorns choke the seed. But the seed which falls on good soil produces abundant fruit and success is achieved at the end. The parable of the growing seed describes how the farmer waits impatiently after the sowing, goes to bed and gets up day after day. The earth produces fruit of itself and one day it is time for harvesting. Finally, the parable of the mustard seed tells of planting one of the smallest seeds; but at the end it is an enormous growth providing shade in which the birds build their nests.

These and similar parables have been given very diverse interpretations. But if they are related to Jesus' work and his preaching of the kingdom of God, it seems reasonable to assume that he is here illustrating the hidden beginning of God's rule and the glorious kingdom of God to be expected at the end—despite all opposition, despite initial insignificance and apparent hopelessness. There is a slightly different emphasis in each parable. The sower is not disappointed in the results of his efforts, since there is a rich yield from the seed that fell on good soil. The farmer can confidently and patiently wait, since he knows that the fruit comes from the hidden forces of the soil: the kingdom of God comes from the power of God. If the beginning is so slight, the end is all the more glorious. In any case, all the stress falls on this expected end: the rich fruit, the welcome harvest, the unpredictable, widespread growth—all this symbolizes the cosmic kingdom of God. Here all that matters to us is the confidence and unshakeable certainty which Jesus reveals in these parables. Is he not himself the sower who decides the beginning and is certain of the happy end? But he is a humble sower, ascribing all the power of growth and all the glory of the consummation to someone else: God, from whom everything proceeds and who brings everything to its end.

When is the kingdom of God coming?

As well as in the growth parables, Jesus has also refuted elsewhere the doubts of his contemporaries. There were certain 'apocalyptic' questions which stirred people at that time: When is the kingdom of God coming? Who will have part in it? Will many be saved? But for Jesus the wish to explore, to calculate, to 'spy out' the future is human curiosity. God goes his own way and it is for us to fulfil the call of the moment. That is also the meaning of the pericope from Luke quoted at the beginning of this chapter. When the Pharisees ask Jesus about the time of the coming of the kingdom, he answers that its coming is not to be observed by signs. In this way he probably intended to reject the desire to calculate in advice with the aid of certain 'portents' the appointed time for the end of this world. People expected extraordinary manifestations in heaven and on earth, menaces which—like flame signals—would draw attention to the end of time. Such oracular signs are not the same things as the 'signs of the time' considered in the first meditation. But human beings are inclined to try to peep behind the curtain of the future. It seems also that primitive Christian groups similarly tried to calculate the end in advance, as the great eschatological discourse in the synoptic Gospels reveals. But the evangelists resisted such temptations and impressed on the communities only alertness and readiness in the Spirit of Jesus. 'You do not know when the master will come' (Mark 13.35); he is coming 'at an unexpected hour' (Luke 12.40).

If today some people discover certain manifestations and events of our own time in the picturesque visions of John's Revelation and want to draw conclusions about the earthly happenings they are to expect, they have not understood the theme of the great book of consolation and warning belonging to the end of the first century. This prophetic book also, making use of forms of style and description current at that time, seeks only to lead the afflicted Christians of Asia Minor to adopt an attitude corresponding to the word and mind of Jesus. It seeks to enable them to withstand the distress of the present time in faith in the coming of their Lord and in trust in God's final victory. In such tribulation what matters is 'the endurance and faith of the saints' (Rev. 13.10).

A reality beginning even now

When the kingdom of God comes, it will not be possible to say: 'Here it is' or 'there'. The future kingdom of God is in no way a factor of earthly-historical reality. Space and time will then have lost their meaning; history will have reached its end. In this negative demarcation from human ideas is contained the clear statement that this kingdom of the consummation is not under men's control and cannot even be imagined by them. It is the consummation of creation brought about by God after all human history and a meaningful close appointed by him to the history of mankind, a new creation in which redeemed humanity finds its ultimate happiness (cf. Rev. 21). In Jesus' words there lies a clear warning against dreaming about it and indulging in yearning desires.

Against the modern background this warning becomes

still more urgent. If we were to take refuge in a meta-historical future, we would lose sight of the present with its troubles and easily evade the tasks assigned to us in our time. Then those despisers of Christianity would be right who accuse us of taking refuge in another world, looking for an unreal future, because we are unable to change conditions in the present world. This is not at all what Jesus intended. Without permitting even the slightest doubt to arise about the future to be brought into effect by God, beyond any future produced by men, he calls us by this very message to action at the present time. People today like to talk about a 'real Utopia': that is, a utopian picture of the future which nevertheless has a relationship to present reality and is even necessary in order to change the latter. If this idea, which germinated in the soil of a different world-view enables us to understand better Jesus' vision of the future, we need not reject it. It does not however get to the core of Jesus' message, since for him the kingdom of God is not merely an idea of the future reaching back into the present, but a reality beginning even now.

Jesus' positive answer runs: 'Behold, the kingdom of God is in the midst of you.' This brief statement has been interpreted in all sorts of ways. Some people thought that it must mean in this context: When the kingdom of God comes, it will be in your midst at one stroke. This idea seems to be confirmed by another saying which follows later in the same section of Luke: 'As the lightning flashes and lights up the sky from one side to the other, so will the Son of man be in his day' (Luke 17.24). But the point here is that Christ's parousia is unpredictable: it is once more a different setting of the question. If our brief statement answers the question when the kingdom of God is coming, it must certainly be referred to the present: the kingdom of God is already in your midst. The fact that it is present here and now and the manner in which it is present make it impossible to calculate its future manifestation.

But what does 'in the midst of you' mean? The Greek expression has again led to a variety of interpretations. The understanding of this as 'within you' had some influence; it would mean that the kingdom of God is a force effective in men. We might think of God's grace or his Spirit, turning men's hearts to good. But the expression 'kingdom of God' is not otherwise used in this sense and it is questionable whether the kingdom of God can be turned into an internal, mental factor—Jesus meant something different. In particular, the translation 'within you' is not supported by the Greek; the expression must be rendered by 'in your midst'. It has been shown too, by closely comparing other passages, that the Greek preposition contains a particularly important meaning. It implies also an appeal to the hearers: The kingdom of God is in your area, it is within your reach, so that you can grasp it and act accordingly.

Call to decision

This idea fits in splendidly with the message of Jesus. Even now God is at work, the signs of his activity are recognizable and they call for a decision. In Jesus' preaching and action God's rule advances into the sphere of men, saving and redeeming, but also calling for and demanding conversion. Jesus is so certain of this that he wants to divert men from all foolish questions about the future and refers them to this present happening. Similarly he answers the question, 'Will those who are saved be few?', with a powerful appeal: 'Strive to enter by the narrow door' (Luke 13.23-4). Jesus opposes apocalyptic dreams and vain questions by the call of the moment, and he does so in the certainty that the future belongs to God.

Most people at that time did not follow Jesus' insistent call. Many perhaps turned away as a result of the frustration of their earthly-political hopes. When Jesus observed the increasing estrangement of the people and the growing hostility of his opponents, he was still not to be deflected from his message. In the supper room he said something to his disciples which reveals his certainty of the coming of the kingdom of God after his death: 'Truly, I say to you, I shall not drink again of the fruit of the vine until that day when I drink it new in the kingdom of God' (Mark 14.25). God knows ways which men do not suspect. Jesus goes to his death; but new hope springs from death. His disciples come to know him as the risen one, as witness and guarantor of the coming world of God. The crucified and risen Christ preaches more loudly than the earthly Jesus could. In faith in him the Church carries with it on its way through human history the indestructible hope sparked off by him.

3   STEADFAST IN AFFLICTION—
     PAUL ON OUR HOPE

We rejoice in our hope of sharing the glory of God.
More than that, we rejoice in our sufferings, knowing
that suffering produces endurance, and endurance produces character, and character produces hope, and hope
does not disappoint us, because God's love has been
poured into our hearts through the Holy Spirit which
has been given to us.

ROMANS 5.2-5

In good times it is not difficult to speak about hope, to
nourish it—as it were—from the experience of success
and advancement. But hope has to be maintained particularly in the midst of distress and affliction, when
clouds darken the way to the future, when a crash is
threatening or severe blows have already thrown us to
the ground. There are not a few documents of early
Christianity which are the fruit of such experiences.
Everywhere there persists the hope established by Jesus
and consolidated by his resurrection, even in fact ripened
to a basic Christian attitude. Nowhere however does it
become so palpable and credible as in the letters of the
Apostle Paul, who experienced as few others all kinds of
affliction and tribulation, bodily suffering, insults and
persecution, reverses and disappointments in his
Churches and yet became the herald of an inconquerable
hope, overcoming all darkness. Hope of final redemption, of union with his Lord, of his own resurrection in
virtue of the power of the spirit already effective, pro-
ceeding from the risen Jesus: this is what sustained him
through all privations and pains, 'fighting without and
fear within' (2 Cor.7.5). 'I consider that the sufferings of

this present time are not worth comparing with the glory that is to be revealed to us' (Rom. 8.18). 'So we do not lose heart. Though our outer nature is wasting away, our inner nature is being renewed every day. For this slight momentary affliction is preparing for us an eternal weight of glory' (2 Cor. 4.16-17).

Hopelessness and the power of Christian hope

We can understand the enormous power of such hope, revealed in human weakness, only when we set against it the sad evidence of the hopelessness prevalent today. Recent statistics show that fatal traffic accidents on the one hand and suicides on the other are increasing at almost the same rate in Western Germany. In fact, while the number of those deprived of life abruptly and involuntarily is slowly declining, the number of those who voluntarily opt out of life is increasing. Apart from the sinister figure of attempted suicides, more than thirteen thousand people put an end to their lives in a single year, many of them being young. Suicide took second place among the causes of death with the fifteen- to twenty-year-olds. It is also well known that not a few who committed suicide were people to whom life offered all that they wanted. But their existence seemed pointless to them. 'I am a nihilist', said the seventeen year old Birthe from Glostrup in Sweden, 'I can't believe in anything. Life is a boring succession of empty days. Sometimes I sit at home and cry—why, I don't know myself. I've got to know everything and it's all stale.'

Hope is part of what is distinctively Christian. It is rooted in faith, which interprets the meaning of life, the riddle of the universe, the darkness of history; and it gathers strength from receiving and giving love, without which there is no meaning in reality. Hope is the sustaining power on life's journey, the characteristic virtue of our earthly-transitory existence. Faith, love, and hope

41

are closely linked together. At one point Paul describes love as the greatest in this triple constellation (1 Cor. 13.13); but when it is a question of the realization of Christian existence in this world, of coping with difficulties, it is hope that is decisive. From the standpoint of our condition in the world the appropriate sequence is faith-love-hope. Faith must become effective in love (Gal. 5.6); from this proceeds the hope of gaining full salvation (cf. Gal. 5.5). The Apostle remembers the Thessalonians with gratitude, since their faith has been proved in action, their love in labour, and their hope in patience (1 Thess. 1.3). After exhortations to love and consideration, he addresses the Romans with his wish and prayer: 'May the God of hope fill you with all joy and peace in believing, so that by the power of the Holy Spirit you may abound in hope' (Rom. 15.13).

But let us turn now to the passage in Romans in which Paul makes Christian hope his special theme (5.1-11). He has previously explained that both Gentiles and Jews are involved in sin and guilt, and all are under God's judgement. Jesus Christ alone has liberated us from sin, since he reconciled mankind with God. Then the Apostle continues: 'Justified by faith, we have peace with God through our Lord Jesus Christ. Through him we have obtained access to this grace in which we stand, and we rejoice in our hope of sharing the glory of God' (5.1-2). With that everything could be said: we have peace now and we hope one day to obtain the fullness of salvation, happiness, and bliss with God. Paul uses for this the expression 'glory': a high-sounding expression in the Bible, but scarcely intelligible to modern men. It is meant to indicate undisturbed participation in God's life with all its splendour, its beauty and joy. Paul will say more about this later, in chapter 8; it is however significant that he does not at once set about describing the content of our hope, but continues in three long chapters to be occupied with the obscurities and difficulties of earthly life. He does not play off a dreamy or emotional view of the future against misery, suffering, and darkness. He looks squarely at this world with its harsh realities and yet ventures to hope. It is not triumphant boasting but a grateful, humble confidence, because he knows that we have obtained peace with God and hope of glory only through Jesus Christ.

Endurance in affliction

Paul turns his gaze almost violently from expected glory to present tribulations, which have to be endured. Steadfastness in earthly afflictions is more important than exulting in future glory. So he continues: 'More than that, we rejoice in our sufferings, knowing that suffering produces endurance . . .' Even suffering and affliction in the world have their meaning. It is only through them that hope develops all its power. In a concise, effective argument he brings the line of thought back again to hope: 'Endurance produces character, and character produces hope.' The hope bestowed however must continually be freshly bought by our own efforts. In enduring earthly tribulations and afflictions the hope inaugurated by God becomes a personal possession. Anyone who accepts hostilities and trials—since we have not yet reached the goal of hope, but are on the road of testing and probation—learns patience, steadfastness, and perseverance. The Greek term translated here by 'endurance' or 'patience' implies much more than the worn-out English expression. It means stamina, standing firm and remaining firm, not a purely 'passive' attitude, but courageous resistance. But this is what produces endurance, an increasing experience that we can sustain trials and burdens. The believer who does not permit himself to be led astray in believing and hoping by any kind of affliction gathers experiences which confirm and strengthen him in his attitude. So hope grows through the resistance it faces. Endurance produces hope, that is, it fills God-given hope, grasped in faith, with new power and certainty.

Despite the brevity of the expression, there is no doubt that these statements embody the rich experience of a man who had to prove his faith existentially. For him, hope is always a 'nevertheless', a 'nevertheless' of course which has its reason in the experience of the love of God. Paul is far from ascribing merit to himself for this steadfastness and unshakeable hope. He knows that all his hope rests on what God has brought to effect in Jesus Christ. It relies on the love which he showed to us when we were still sinners (v.8). 'If while we were enemies we were reconciled to God by the death of his Son, much more, now that we are reconciled, shall we be saved by his life' (v.10). Paul knows however that this love of God has become deeply rooted in his heart and that is the true reason of his unshakeable hope. 'Hope does not disappoint us, because God's love has been poured into our hearts through the Holy Spirit which has been given to us' (v.5).

That is why Paul speaks of the 'God of hope'; without him his hope would break down. As Jesus expected the coming kingdom of God, not as a result of human proficiency and prudence, but from God's power and wisdom, so Paul also in the midst of tribulation and distress places his whole trust in God. But hope has now acquired a new perspective; through Jesus' death and resurrection it has a clearer view of the future consummation. Jesus' immediacy to God his Father gave him the unshakeable certainty that God's now perceptible rule will prevail, despite all opposition. In the raising up of the Crucified, Paul does not see merely the confirmation of Jesus' idea of God; for him it is also God's decisive act which guarantees and brightly illuminates the future. The risen Christ is himself the guarantor of the coming world of God. Christ 'was crucified in weakness, but lives by the power of God' (2 Cor. 13.4), and this living Christ is the 'first-born among many brethren' (Rom. 8.29). Looking to this crucified and risen Christ, Paul sees that on earth he must take on himself the suffering of his Lord, even to the point of death, in order one day to share in his life. 'For while we live we are always being given up to death for Jesus' sake, so that the life of Jesus may be manifested in our mortal flesh' (2 Cor. 4.11). So the afflictions and sufferings which he has to bear as Apostle of Jesus Christ become for him the seal of his belonging to Christ, the sign that his hope too will be fulfilled. 'That I may know [Christ] and the power of his resurrection, and may share his sufferings, becoming like him in his death, that if possible I may attain the resurrection from the dead' (Phil. 3.10-11).

Flight from earthly joys?

This passionate acceptance of tribulation and suffering for Christ's sake might seem exaggerated to us. Does it not lead to a craving for suffering and a flight from earthly joys which is unnatural and unhealthy? Is it not a rejection of creation with its beauty and all that it offers for man's happiness? Is the Christian not to be allowed to rejoice in this world?

We should misunderstand Paul if we were to draw these conclusions from the passages quoted from his letters. Careful reading of his letters shows how much he too was interested in joy and how tirelessly he sought to impart joy. His main concern of course was with joy as the fruit of the Holy Spirit. 'The kingdom of God is not food and drink but righteousness and peace and joy in the Holy Spirit' (Rom. 14.17). But in fact the painful experiences are predominant in the hard life of this missionary and champion of Christ. His own experience then forces him to reflect on the meaning of the sufferings which—despite his gospel of reconciliation and peace, of freedom and joy—still accompany the course of world-history and burden the life of men.

Paul knows that the burden of suffering laid on him, the Apostle of Jesus Christ, is not laid on all Christians. But, by uniting himself to the sufferings of his Lord, he does a great service to all; he shows that afflictions and sufferings also belong to this world, and we cannot thrust them out of our consciousness. They must be mastered by being accepted and their meaning recognized. Paul teaches this not only in words, but also by the example of his own person. In Corinth there were zealots who considered themselves already perfect because of their possession of the Spirit and boasted of their strength. Paul writes to them: 'Already you are filled! Already you have become rich! Without us you have become kings!' Then he puts before their eyes the wretched lives of the apostles:

> I think that God has exhibited us apostles as last of all, like men sentenced to death; because we have become a spectacle to the world, to angels and to men. We are fools for Christ's sake, but you are wise in Christ. We are weak, but you are strong. You are held in honor, but we in disrepute. To the present hour we hunger and thirst, we are ill-clad and buffeted and homeless, and we labor, working with our own hands. When reviled, we bless; when persecuted, we endure (1 Cor. 4.8-12).

The irony with which Paul tries to rouse these Christians is unmistakable, and yet behind it is a deep seriousness. The latter forget that we may not withdraw from this world with its misery, that following Christ in his sufferings is precisely a part of Christian existence. As long as this world exists, pains and sufferings are unavoidable; we must accept them 'for Christ's sake', who accepted his sufferings for our sake.

Acceptance of one's own suffering means also identify-
ing with suffering mankind. After being rescued from a
great affliction, which brought him to the brink of
death, Paul writes to the Corinthians:

> Blessed be the God and Father of our Lord Jesus
> Christ, the Father of mercies and God of all comfort;
> who comforts us in all our affliction, so that we may
> be able to comfort those who are in any affliction,
> with the comfort with which we ourselves are com-
> forted by God. For as we share abundantly in Christ's
> sufferings, so through Christ we share abundantly in
> comfort too. If we are afflicted, it is for your com-
> fort . . . which you experience when you patiently
> endure the same sufferings that we suffer. Our hope
> for you is unshaken; for we know that as you share in
> our sufferings, you will also share in our comfort
> (2 Cor. 1.3-7).

Experience of suffering has taught the Apostle to understand himself even better as a man, but also to understand other human beings in their needs. For himself he
admits frankly: 'We were so utterly, unbearably crushed
that we despaired of life itself'; but then he continues:
'Why, we felt that we had received the sentence of death;
but that was to make us rely not on ourselves but on God
who raises the dead; he delivered us from so deadly a
peril, and he will deliver us; on him we have set our hope
that he will deliver us again' (1.8-10). But Paul is thinking also of the needs of other people and longs 'to comfort those who are in any affliction, with the comfort
with which we ourselves are comforted by God' (1.4).

Whatever was the peril of death which faced Paul in
the Province of Asia—some scholars think it was a serious
illness, others persecution and external affliction—the
ideas he links with it ensure a deep insight into his

47

human and Christian attitude. These statements, in which the immediate experience reverberates, confirm the fact that there is a personal experience of the Apostle behind the brief formulation in Romans 5: 'Suffering produces endurance and endurance produces character, and character produces hope.' Prayer too comes within this range of experience: prayer of petition in distress and prayer of thanksgiving after rescue. In order to gain further protection Paul invites the Corinthians: 'You also must help us by prayer, so that many will give thanks on our behalf for the blessing granted us' (1.11). Paul then is not using empty phrases when he appeals to the Romans in another context: 'Rejoice in your hope, be patient in tribulation, be constant in prayer' (12.12).

Existence in tension

Paul, who as a Christian has committed his life wholly to Jesus Christ crucified and risen and yet as a man remains involved in earthly reality, lives in a continual and irremovable tension. His faith that he has obtained justification and peace, true freedom and peace in Jesus Christ, continually comes up against the harsh realities in this world. The hope of final and definitive salvation, emerging from faith, because creation is still unredeemed and even the Christian is exposed to temptations, is continually subjected to severe tests. But, particularly in this intense struggle for a religious understanding of the world and a Christian attitude to the world, Paul will attract many modern men. Is there not even now something enigmatic and contradictory about the world which is accessible to us and which we experience? It is a wonderful world continually revealing to us new beauties, hidden forces and more or less inexhaustible riches, and yet a world in which there are pain and destruction, the 'groaning' of the creature, sickness and death.

And in it there is man, this glorious and proud creature, equipped with great mental power, able to cultivate his living space, capable of good deeds in human society, and yet also plunged in misery, bodily and mental distress, consciously bearing all kinds of burdens, with an incomprehensible propensity to evil, creating unhappiness for himself and others. The times when people felt secure in the order of nature and in the developed systems of social life—if they ever existed—have gone for ever. There are many who suffer from anxiety about the future and from existential fear. They will understand Paul in his suffering in the darkness and misery of the world and in his trials caused by the wickedness and malice of men. His language and mode of thought, however, which tie him to his own time, may not always be intelligible to them.

Paul sees as dangerous and destructive powers those menacing and depressing things which darken human life and prevent man from truly fulfilling his human existence. After the chapter (Rom. 5) on the prospect of final salvation under the heading of 'hope', he goes on (Rom. 6—8) to name the powers of evil which work together for man's ruin. For the Christian, thanks to the redemption through Jesus Christ, they are powers now overcome, and yet he continues to encounter them in the world and is exposed to their attack. This is especially true of the power of sin, which inwardly enslaves man, makes him a prisoner, and delivers him up to death, to that final death which consists in God's judgement on a sinful and misspent life: an annihilating end. The Christian is freed from the power of sin and should no longer submit to its control (Rom. 6).

Paul is also occupied with the law which leads to bondage, sin, and death, and finally with death as the power of evil *par excellence*. Paul's way of thinking in terms of 'powers' creates difficulties for us, and yet we can share in his feeling of being inwardly shattered by the sinister forces in the world and in man's heart. 'Wretched man that I am! Who will deliver me from this body of death? Thanks be to God through Jesus Christ our Lord! . . . For the law of the Spirit of life in Christ Jesus has set me free from the law of sin and death' (Rom. 7.24-5, 8.2).

Being led by the Spirit

In face of the fragility of human nature and the transitoriness of all earthly things, with Paul hope always breaks through as the sun's rays break through dark clouds. Inevitable death, which deeply depresses man, loses its terror for him because of his hope of the resurrection. 'If the Spirit of him who raised Jesus from the dead dwells in you, he who raised Christ Jesus from the dead will give life to your mortal bodies also through his Spirit which dwells in you' (8.11). But the divine Spirit of life bestowed on us does not relieve us of the burden of moral effort. 'If you live according to the flesh you will die, but if by the Spirit you put to death the deeds of the body you will live' (8.13).

What Paul calls 'the flesh' is not the body with its natural needs, but man with his evil inclinations. Anyone who gives way to them, makes them the norm of his action, is on the way to that death which is not merely the end of physical life, but also means missing life's true goal; it is man's final eclipse. But we have within us another principle of life, which Paul calls the divine 'Spirit'; this Spirit of God is granted to us and planted in us through our union with Christ, the risen and living one. 'God's love has been poured into our hearts through the Holy Spirit which has been given to us' (5.5). Anyone who orients his life in the light of the Spirit and puts to death 'the deeds of the body' will live. He will rise to that life in which the love he has received and sown finds its supreme fulfilment. Hope of living on with God or—

better—the consummation of human life in God, the fullness of life, is rooted for Paul in the resurrection of the Crucified.

What we call today man's 'transcendental destiny', that striving of man for an ultimate fulfilment of meaning which his earthly existence cannot offer him, is absolutely sure for Paul as for Jesus and forms the presupposition of his message of hope. 'If for this life only we have hoped in Christ, we are of all men most to be pitied' (1 Cor. 15.19). It is the same view which Jesus puts forward: 'What does it profit a man, to gain the whole world and forfeit his life?' (Mark 8.36): that is, what use is it to a man if he misses the true goal of his life, loses the life which is peculiar to him and leads to God? Perhaps for us modern men this life will be more comprehensible if we understand it with Paul as life filled with the love of God and arousing us to love, to a love which longs for greater and more lasting fulfilment.

The grandeur of hope

Paul's exhortation to live according to the norm and promptings of the Holy Spirit within us leads to the great passage in which he takes up again the theme of hope and now reveals its content more fully. He starts out from what is bestowed on us in Jesus Christ and concludes from this to what we have still to expect. The divine Spirit in us bears witness that we are children of God and, if children, then heirs also: heirs of God and co-heirs with Christ (8.16-17). The present experience of being children of God—which itself means liberation from anxiety and fear, since we appeal trustfully to God, our Father—permits us to surmise what the full sonship of God will mean, which is to be revealed to us. For then we shall be liberated also from the bondage of transience, from the sufferings of the present time, from our weakness and frailty, our liability to death. We have received only the initial gift of the Spirit and may hope for its fullness and glory.

Even Paul cannot describe concretely the happiness and bliss of our complete redemption; here human language, which remains tied to our earthly-historical world of experience, is bound to fail. Paul is aware of this when he writes: 'In this hope we were saved. Now hope that is seen is not hope. For who hopes for what he sees? But if we hope for what we do not see, we wait for it with patience' (8.24-5). So Paul finds himself thrown back once more on 'patience', steadfast perseverance. The tension is inescapable: from present affliction we turn our attention to what faith knows to be the certain future, the future which will bring final liberation, un-clouded happiness, love without end. But if the Christian wants to settle down there in his thoughts and to seek consolation there, he will be continually called back into the present: not only by its harsh realities, but also by the special character of his hope which demands from him steadfastness and perseverance at the present time.

Redemption of creation

These statements, giving expression to intensive reflec-tion on Christian existence in this world, refute the charge that Christian hope incites people to flight from earthly reality. Christians who do attempt such a retreat have wrongly understood the message of faith. This holds too for an individualistic, narrow-minded piety, centred on our own ego. Paul thinks on a cosmic scale, as this very passage in Romans 8 reveals. For he brings the rest of creation into his vision of 'the glory that is to be revealed to us' (8.18).

'The creation was subjected to futility, not of its own will but by the will of him who subjected it in hope; be-cause the creation itself will be set free from its bondage to decay and obtain the glorious liberty of the children of God' (vv. 20-1). The language and presentation in these verses strike us as peculiar and strange. Then we even read that, together with us, 'the whole creation has been groaning in travail' (v. 22). These are the kind of expressions and metaphors encountered in Jewish apocalyptic writings, talking of creation in a human way, in a consideration of the world concentrated on man. It is also difficult to determine the exact meaning of individual phrases, which are very diversely interpreted. But the relationship of creation to man and the incorporation of man into the cosmos draw attention to an important and essential preoccupation: Paul is concerned with the future of mankind, with its final hope, which it shares with the rest of creation. Human life and human history are not realized in isolation from the world which surrounds man.

At a time of environmental pollution, exploitation of natural resources, perceptible changes in our living space, we may perhaps understand this better than formerly. What matters to us here is the cosmic vision of the Apostle. He certainly does not want to say anything directly on the future destiny of the cosmos: that is, nothing on whether there will be a universal catastrophe or whether the world will continue to exist in a different form. But he sees man's destiny as intertwined with that of the world, which is his living space, and he has also hope for this world. In a comprehensive interpretation of human history, his survey reaches from the beginning of creation to its consummation. Creation and redemption cannot be separated from one another.

Secure in God's love

Again the modern sceptics will ask what use such a religious consideration of the world is supposed to be for the accumulating problems of mankind's future. But, as long as history is made by men, what matters is that there is a bright sky above all dark clouds, a recognizable meaning behind all possible developments, no threat of final extinction despite all depressing experiences. This hope Paul cherishes; at the close of his far-reaching and pregnant reflections, he again gives it powerful expression.

On what does he base his incontestable certainty? First of all on the Holy Spirit who comes to the aid of our weakness, when we are depressed by the 'groaning of the creature' in us and want to groan ourselves and give way to despondency. The Spirit takes up our groaning—so to speak—and carries it to God, and God 'who searches the hearts of men knows what is the mind of the Spirit' (8.27). This is Paul's profound experience of prayer, from which his assurance breaks forth: 'We know that in everything God works for good with those who love him' (8.28). So in the last resort it is the God of hope in whom the Christian places his confidence. God, who has called us, will also lead us to fulfilment. 'If God is for us, who is against us?' God has proved that he is for us by the fact that 'he did not spare his own Son but gave him up for us all; will he not also give us all things with him?' We have already experienced the supreme proof of God's love and therefore need no longer fear anything. In Jesus Christ the love of God has been made evident to us; in the love of Christ we are certain of God's love.

> Who shall separate us from the love of Christ? Shall tribulation, or distress, or persecution, or famine, or nakedness, or peril, or sword? As it is written,
> 'For thy sake we are being killed all the day long;
> we are regarded as sheep to be slaughtered.'
> No, in all these things we are more than conquerors through him who loved us. For I am sure that neither death, nor life, nor angels, nor principalities, nor things present, nor things to come, nor powers, nor

height, nor depth, nor anything else in all creation, will be able to separate us from the love of God in Christ Jesus our Lord (8.35-9).

This hymn of hope, to which Paul rises at the end, speaks for itself. It is the testimony of a man who has suffered almost more than any other from the darkness of the world and the abysses of human existence and yet, liberated by Christ, has struggled through in freedom to this hope. Recalling once again the signs of the time, we can see that for him the very sufferings of the time have become signals which put him on the alert. Behind all afflictions and sufferings there is a hidden salvific will of God which becomes visible in the mission of his Son. In the suffering of his Son God conquers the suffering of the world. Looking to the crucified Christ, whom God has raised up, there is for Paul a 'hope against hope', that is, a hope in the God 'who gave life to the dead and calls into existence the things that do not exist' (Rom. 4.17).

4 FORCES OF THE FUTURE AT THE PRESENT TIME— THE JOHANNINE VISION

If you abide in me, and my words abide in you, ask whatever you will, and it shall be done for you. By this my Father is glorified, that you bear much fruit, and so prove to be my disciples. As the Father has loved me, so have I loved you; abide in my love. If you keep my commandments, you will abide in my love, just as I have kept my Father's commandments and abide in his love. These things I have spoken to you, that my joy may be in you, and that your joy may be full.

JOHN 15.7-11

In primitive Christianity the Christian attitude to the world took on a variety of forms. Paul was a quick-tempered man, a fighter, inwardly agitated, burning with missionary zeal, who mastered all difficulties by his deep faith and passionate love for Christ, who never gave up hope and pressed on unswervingly 'for the prize of the upward call of God in Christ Jesus' (Phil. 3.14). To the tension and unrest of his outward life corresponds his pregnant, penetrating, occasionally erratic thinking, which never seems to reach a final adjustment. If we pass from his letters to the Johannine writings—the Gospel and letters of John—we are in the midst of a quite different atmosphere. If we wanted to compare the two, we might say that Paul works like a foaming mountain torrent, rushing to its goal with elemental force, while John resembles a clear, calm lake, sparkling in the sun, with scarcely a ripple on the surface, hinting at unfathomable depths. But all comparisons break down: we are faced

with different ways of thinking and talking, which—
despite their common faith in Christ—reveal different
attitudes to the world and men.

John too—as we shall call the personality behind the
last of the four Gospels, whose identity is disputed—has
exercised a great influence by his proclamation of Christ.
He gathered a group of disciples around him and informed
with his spirit communities of which we know very little
but which established themselves in their milieu and in
the intellectual trends of their time. We can speak of a
'Johannine Christianity'. The historical influence of the
Johannine writings and the theology contained in them
was even more permanent. Their profound understanding of the person of Jesus Christ and their interpretation
of his message have stimulated and enriched Christian
faith and Christian piety throughout the ages. Even today
the language of the Johannine Christ can touch us directly.
But what of the view of the world, of mankind, of the
future?

Involvement in the world or flight from the world?

It has been said that John stands for an unworldly Christianity, that he regards the world as something completely negative and wants to isolate from it the community
of the 'elect'. The community—it is claimed—lacks
awareness of history and a sense of responsibility for
mankind; it withdraws into its own way of life and finds
its sufficiency in fellowship with God and fraternal
solidarity; it is a community occupied with mysteries,
isolated from the world. If this were true, then Johannine Christianity would certainly have little meaning for
us today; but it would also be very remote from the
intention of Jesus. Since however we do not know the
Johannine community directly, but are dependent on
inference from the Gospel and the letters, the impression
of a complete aversion from the world and a decisive

retreat into the inner life—which may be gained from some passages—can be deceptive and conceal the real attitude of Johannine Christianity. The words quoted above, from the farewell discourses, are not meant only for the disciples in the supper room, but are addressed also to the later community for its life of faith and its moral effort, and are linked also to a particular standpoint. The inner encouragement which the community receives through the words of Jesus is directed to this particular situation and does not explain everything which stirs the community and all that it seeks.

The community addressed is in a depressed state and has to put up with molestation and persecution. This emerges from the following passage in which Jesus seeks to strengthen and console the disciples in face of the world's hatred and persecutions by men: 'If the world hates you, know that it has hated me before it hated you. If you were of the world, the world would love its own; but because you are not of the world, but I chose you out of the world, therefore the world hates you. Remember the word that I said to you, "A servant is not greater than his master." If they persecuted me, they will persecute you' (John 15.18-20).

People who are under great pressure need to be encouraged and to build up their self-assurance if they are to stand firm. It was all the more difficult for the Christians of the Johannine community because their opponents were evidently Jews who persecuted them for religious motives. 'They will put you out of the synagogues; indeed, the hour is coming when whoever kills you will think he is offering service to God' (16.2). As a result of this, Christians who came from Judaism might easily lose their feeling of security. They were subjected to the same religiously inspired contempt as that which Jesus faced, being finally delivered up by the leaders of the Jewish people to a shameful death on the cross.

John's Gospel as a whole reflects the conflict between early Christianity and the influential Judaism of the hellenistic cities outside Palestine, whether in Syria or Asia Minor. It is understandable that it was important in such a situation to make Christians aware that they were following the true faith, that they were chosen and loved by God. Jesus is the true vine, planted by God, and they are to regard themselves as branches on this vine (15.1 and 5).

It is then very remarkable how the Johannine community is exhorted to behave in this depressed state. It is not to react with hatred to the world's hatred, but must show by its love and by producing fruit that it belongs to God and is the community of Jesus' disciples. By living according to God's will and realizing the instructions of Jesus—especially the commandment of love—it is to bear witness before the 'world' and convince the latter of the truth of faith in Christ. Can this be expressed more beautifully and more clearly than in Jesus' great prayer in the supper room on parting from his disciples?

> That they all may be one: even as thou, Father, art in me, and I in thee, that they also may be in us, so that the world may believe that thou hast sent me. The glory which thou hast given me I have given to them, that they may be one even as we are one, I in them and thou in me, that they may become perfectly one, so that the world may know that thou hast sent me and hast loved them even as thou hast loved me (17.21-3).

This passage is often quoted to emphasize the fact that the idea of unity among separated Christians was a pressing concern of Jesus and to stimulate ecumenical agreement between the Churches. Important as this is in the present situation of the world and although it can and must be drawn as a conclusion from Jesus' parting prayer, the original intention in regard to the Johannine community was different. That community was to show forth God's nature and character, as represented in the unity of Jesus with God, being drawn by Jesus into the unity and fellowship of God, and this was to be a testimony to a world remote from God. The Johannine community was not filled with the missionary zeal and activism of Paul; but it sought by its very existence and the form of its existence, by its life, its love, its fraternal fellowship, to be a sign of God in this world and to convince men of the love of God which has been fulfilled in the mission of his Son.

Inner penetration of the world

Certainly this appears to be a passive attitude, an inward trend—but must it be a retreat into the ghetto? It cannot be denied that this danger existed, and we do not know whether those communities in their particular situation were not to some extent exposed to it. But there are signs that they remained nevertheless aware of their task in the world and of their responsibility for the world. The Johannine Christ too says to his disciples on Easter evening: 'As the Father has sent me, even so I send you' (20.21), and he prays for them: 'I do not pray that thou shouldst take them out of the world, but that thou shouldst keep them from the evil one . . . Sanctify them in the truth; thy word is truth. As thou didst send me into the world, so I have sent them into the world. And for their sake I consecrate myself, that they also may be consecrated in truth' (17.15, 17-19). This is simply a different approach to the 'mission to the world', stressing not so much missionary activity as permeating the world with God's salvific powers.

This is not to say that traces of external missionary activity are entirely lacking. In a conversation in Samaria Jesus tells his disciples: 'I sent you to reap that for which you did not labor; others have labored, and you have

entered into their labor' (4.38). Who are these 'others'?
Very probably early Christian missionaries of whose
efforts the community is being reminded. In the third
Johannine letter the author invites Gaius, the recipient,
to support these itinerant missionaries who are highly
praised for their selfless work. 'So we ought to support
such men, that we may be fellow workers in the truth'
(3 John 8). The times are now different from those in
which Paul and other men first set out to carry the
message of Christ to the world and to found communities. Not a few Christian communities are now looking
back over a longer existence, their life has become
settled; but they are faced by new problems: hostility
from outside and already disruptions within (1 John
2.18f.), moral lapses on the part of members of the
community, slackening zeal. It is only by recalling all
this that we can begin to grasp the importance of what is
said in the Johannine writings to the communities.

Abiding in Jesus

In these writings there is one word which occurs more
frequently than anywhere else in the New Testament,
more than four times as often as in the Pauline letters:
this is 'remain' or 'abide'. The passage from the farewell
discourses, on which we are basing our meditation, also
begins with the invitation to abide in Jesus. It is the basic
theme of the previous discourse on the vine: 'Abide in
me, and I in you. As the branch cannot bear fruit by itself, unless it abides in the vine, neither can you, unless
you abide in me' (15.4). The Johannine community can
hold its own and prove its worth only if it clings firmly
to what it has been given and abides in it. And what is
this gift? In the longer letter a great deal is mentioned
which is 'in' the believers or which they 'have': the truth
(2.4), the word of God (2.14), the 'anointing'—a metaphor for the Holy Spirit—(2.27), 'God's seed' (3.9), his

61

life (3.15), his love (3.17; 4.12). We might continue from the Gospel: the Spirit of truth (14.17), the peace of Christ (14.27), his joy (15.11), and continually the divine life. In the last resort it is a question of 'fellowship . . . with the Father and with his Son Jesus Christ' (1 John 1.3), being taken up into God and his life or—from a different standpoint—of God's coming and dwelling with men (cf. John 14.23), the infusion of divine vital forces in men. Where God is, he is present with his life and light, his truth, his love, his joy.

John is never tired of proclaiming that this fellowship with God was bestowed on us by Jesus Christ, his Son. 'In this the love of God was made manifest among us, that God sent his only Son into the world, so that we might live through him' (1 John 4.9). This Son, sent into the world, can say of himself: 'I am the light of the world; he who follows me will not walk in darkness, but will have the light of life' (John 8.12). 'He who has seen me has seen the Father' (14.9); 'he who loves me will be loved by my Father' (14.21). For the community, then, only one thing is necessary: to remain in Jesus and through him to remain in God. 'If what you heard from the beginning abides in you, then you will abide in the Son and in the Father' (1 John 2.24).

This is a different outlook from that of Paul, who indeed is profoundly convinced of his present fellowship with Christ his Lord and stirred by this (Gal. 2.20), but at the same time looks longingly for his coming in power, for the parousia. In John this tension has perceptibly disappeared. The frequent use of 'abide' as a reminder and an exhortation betokens a different basic mood, a conscience fully aware of the demands of the present time, a striving for steadfastness. John's is a contemplative nature; he reflects on the existing situation, sees things as they really are, and finds in the truth revealed by Jesus Christ the answer to all obscure and urgent questions. For he too by no means fails to see the darkness and evil in the world; on the contrary, 'the world' appears to him as the realm of darkness and of death. He contrasts it sharply with the realm of light and life, the divine realm, from which Jesus comes and into which he leads those who believe in him.

This is 'dualism', a way of thinking in pairs of opposites which are assigned to two opposite realms, an outlook widely spread at the time. Johannine dualism is spatially oriented: the 'lower' world of sin and death is opposed to the 'upper' world of God. On one occasion in John's Gospel Jesus tells those who are stubbornly hostile: 'You are from below, I am from above; you are of this world, I am not of this world. I told you that you would die in your sins' (8.23-4). We moderns may find this idea of an upper and lower world disconcerting and irritating, but we should not overlook the fact that for John it was the only one possible and acceptable mode of expression, fitting in with the view of the world at that time, to describe redemption from all types of disaster and evil. Jesus, who comes 'from above', from God's world, leads those who believe in him out of the calamity of sin and death. The Son of God, united with God the Father, says: 'He who hears my word and believes him who sent me, has eternal life; he does not come into judgment, but has passed from death to life' (5.24), that is, even now, in this world. The spatial idea, which is clearly expressed here, is merely an outward form of presentation.

Pray for everything

During the First World War Walter Flex, a young man, disillusioned by the cruel events of war and shocked by this world of dread and terror, wrote a small book called *Wanderer between Two Worlds*. He used the same metaphor of the two worlds to express his longing for another world which is still unspoilt and serene. We need not look beyond the stars for God's world, that spiritual-transcendent world to which we are drawn by our mind, our striving and longing, but can discover it in the depths of the visible and palpable world. Following that discovery does not necessarily imply weakness and flight: it may be the only way of enduring a desolate world. Flex writes in a poem:

> Prayer means burying ourselves in God
> and from God to rise to life.

Another Christian thinker who struggled passionately with the darkness and misery of the world, the Frenchman Leon Bloy, describes his experience in this way:

> We must pray, in order to endure the horror of this world.
> We must pray, in order to be pure.
> We must pray, in order to obtain strength to wait.
> For the man who prays there is neither despair nor bitter sadness.

In John's Gospel Jesus says to his disciples: 'If you abide in me, and my words abide in you, ask whatever you will, and it shall be done for you' (15.7). This great promise, which occurs repeatedly in the farewell discourses, certainly does not refer to ordinary, earthly things, but to all that is connected with being a disciple: endurance in the world, producing fruit in love, unity, and brotherliness, continuation of the work of Jesus. For the relationship to the world and behaviour in the world, prayer is the centre of recollection, creative force, the new start, as we learn from Jesus' life. The promise that prayer will be heard, to which Johannine Christianity clings, is likewise found already in the Synoptic Gospels.

Producing rich fruit

Prayer and worship however are not the only things which

this community has at heart. It is by no means absorbed in mysticism or in thoughts of the mysteries, but is called to moral effort to produce fruit. This is such a conspicuous feature, especially in the longer letter, that something characteristic of the striving and the specific life of this community must be revealed in it. This writing contains an attack on others who actually sought only knowledge of God, vision of God, union with God, and neglected love of the brethren: 'He who says "I know him" but disobeys his commandments is a liar, and the truth is not in him; but whoever keeps his word, in him truly love for God is perfected . . . he who says he abides in him ought to walk in the same way in which he [Jesus Christ] walked' (1 John 2.4-6). Moral perseverance is the touchstone of a genuine quest for God; brotherly love is a distinguishing feature of Christianity. That group of fanatical Christians which formerly belonged to the community has set itself apart in the meantime. 'They went out from us, but they were not of us; for if they had been of us, they would have continued with us' (2.19).

On the discourse to the disciples in the supper room we read: 'By this my Father is glorified, that you bear much fruit, and so prove to be my disciples' (John 15.8). Producing fruit is the real point of the discourse on the vine. The metaphor of Jesus as the vine and the disciples as the branches on it has often been 'mystically' interpreted. It has been suggested that the idea of the tree of life recurs here. The divine bringer of life is said to impart permanent divine life to all who are associated with him. In reality it is a question of the disciples producing fruit. It is true that abiding in Christ is the presupposition for this, but the intention is to exhort and encourage the disciples to a 'fruitful' life. That is why from the very beginning God is introduced as the wine-grower intent on producing rich fruit by carefully cultivating the vine. He cuts off any branch which produces no fruit and prunes any branch which does produce fruit, so that it will produce even more (v.2). It is not easy to say whether 'pruning', cutting off dead or wild shoots, refers to anything definite. It has been interpreted as the trials and sufferings of the disciples or even as painful renunciation and penance. In any case the discourse takes up at the end once more God's intention to obtain rich fruit. Anyone who wants to become or prove himself to be a disciple must show this in his whole life in the fruits which he produces.

What is meant by these fruits? Moral perseverance in the widest sense, especially in love, which for John becomes the essential and even the sole commandment, which includes all the rest. It is true that Jesus speaks of his 'commandments' in the plural, but he sums them up in the one commission: 'This is my commandment, that you love one another as I have loved you' (15.12).

Love received and given

We need not explain in detail the requirement of love which is unmistakably inculcated in John in all its tremendous force in the light of the example of Jesus. But we may ask what it means for the community's understanding of itself and for its attitude to the world. First of all it is quite clear that the community is aware of its capacity for brotherly love in virtue of the love it has received from God.

Psychologists and educationists today are agreed on the fact that a person's capacity for love can be awakened and strengthened only if he himself receives love. If a basic trust is not awakened in the child, he remains without that which is most important for his later development. If the growing person has not experienced any security with someone who loves him, he turns to aggression and unsocial behaviour. If his trust in other people is continually shaken and disappointed, his relationship to his milieu is disturbed. This essentially simple truth, which modern studies of development and behaviour merely confirm and deepen, is contained in Jesus' words: 'As the Father has loved me, so have I loved you; abide in my love' (15.9). The believer knows that he is secure in the love of Jesus and the Father and all that he has to trouble about is contained in the one statement: 'Abide in my love.' But, in order to abide in the love of Jesus—this must be expressly stated once more—it is necessary 'to keep his commandments', that is, to fulfil the one commandment he imposes on the disciples: to love one another. They are to pass on to the brethren the love they have received from Jesus.

If we consider what this basic attitude means for the present time and for future society, we can see what a decisive contribution Johannine Christianity makes to the mastery of mankind's problems today. For what is the use of all external measures and planning to overcome distress and hunger in the world, to avoid violent conflicts, to secure peace among the nations, if the inclination to aggression, oppression of others, brutal self-assertion in men themselves, is not broken down and the will to mutual aid awakened? It is true that many people today make efforts of this kind purely out of a humane attitude and because they see that otherwise there is no future for mankind; but for Christians, whose faith shows them the right direction, the requirement of brotherly love is more deeply rooted and more firmly established in their attitude of belief. 'We know and believe the love God has for us. God is love, and he who abides in love abides in God, and God abides in him' (1 John 4.16).

Love means serving

The Johannine community wanted to abide in God and in his love by practising love according to Jesus' instruction, 'not in word or speech, but in deed and in truth'

(3.18). In their conditions of life all this was involved in fraternal fellowship. Can we conclude from the absence of the requirement to love neighbours and enemies that the community wanted to restrict Jesus' commandment of love to the group of brethren? When there was a question of active love, the community, in which there were poor, weak, and fainthearted, was the immediate field of action. If it is not to become mere lip-service or a lie, love must be proved in the concrete situation. This community, seeking to live by the love of God, had as its model Jesus' love for his disciples. 'As I have loved you': this reminded them of Jesus washing the disciples' feet at the Last Supper. The repeated exhortations to brotherly love in the farewell discourses look back to that event. 'If I then, your Lord and Teacher, have washed your feet, you also ought to wash one another's feet. For I have given you an example, that you also should do as I have done to you' (John 13.14-15). Jesus' action illustrates the fact that love means serving, humbling oneself before inferiors, being devoted to others.

As John sees it, washing the disciples' feet reveals something more: it is a sign of the death of Jesus. This supreme proof of his love is also continually in the mind of the community. 'By this we know love, that he laid down his life for us; and we ought to lay down our lives for the brethren' (1 John 3.16). But since this will remain an exception, the sober facts of ordinary life must now be considered. 'If any one has the world's goods and sees his brother in need, yet closes his heart against him, how does God's love abide in him?' (3.17). This solid realism refutes the charge that the Johannine community is living remote from the world, in blissful union with God. 'No man has ever seen God; if we love one another, God abides in us and his love is perfected in us' (4.12): this is the attitude of those Christians.

Love is increasing light

In the light of Jesus' example and instruction practical love becomes for the Johannine community also a sign of the fact that God's light sends its rays into the dark world. The author of the letter reminds his readers of the old and yet new commandment of which they are aware: an old commandment since they have heard it from the beginning and yet a new commandment 'which is true in him and in you, because the darkness is passing away and true light is already shining' (1 John 2.8). This statement, at first difficult to understand, permits us however to look deeply into the way in which the community sees itself. With the love which he taught, lived, and sealed with his death, Jesus brought something new into the world, made a light shine which drives out darkness, a light that will never fade. For he continues to live in his community and is active through it; hence it is said: 'in him and in you'. This bold statement seems almost shocking. The revelation and reality of the love which came into the world with Jesus continues in the community. But we find the same thing in another text: 'We know that we have passed out of death into life, because we love the brethren' (3.14). A noble self-awareness, which however is constantly linked with the exhortation to realize love in deed and truth.

The power which opens a way into the future

'The darkness is passing away and true light is already shining' (2.8). Thus we learn something finally about the attitude of Johannine Christianity towards the future. These Christians too see the present world still filled with darkness and men worried by hatred and evil desires; but what is dark and evil must yield to the increasing power of the light. The evangelist represents Jesus' 'exaltation' on the cross as a victory over the 'ruler of the world': 'Now is the judgment of this world, now shall the ruler of this world be cast out; and I, when I am lifted up from the earth, will draw all men to myself' (John 12.31-2). The author of the letter writes at the end: 'We know that . . . the whole world is in the power of the evil one. And we know that the Son of God has come and has given us understanding, to know him who is true [that is, God]' (1 John 5.19-20), and in another text: 'He who is in you is greater than he who is in the world' (4.4). Despite all the power of evil, God remains the stronger; this is guaranteed by the Son of God, who has come into the world, and by his victory on the cross. God's vital forces, his light and his love, have flowed into the world and continue to be active there. The community is convinced of this, since it is aware of these forces present and effective in itself. If we understand John rightly, then the love which came into the world with Jesus is for him that power which overcomes all the power of evil and opens into the future a way which will never end in destruction.

Joy from the presence of Christ

This knowledge bestowed by faith permits us to overcome all sadness and hopelessness and leads to a joy which emerges from within us to permeate the whole of life. The sayings of Jesus which we have chosen culminate in the statement: 'These things I have spoken to you, that my joy may be in you, and that your joy may be full' (John 15.11). It is not an exuberant zest for living, but a silent joy, creating inward warmth, a joy too that is not a kind of euphoric mood turning easily into depression. It is a lasting joy, announced by Jesus as he leaves his disciples, which will begin with Easter: 'I will see you again and your hearts will rejoice, and no one will take your joy from you' (16.22). Here is revealed a basic mood of Johannine Christianity: a mood which may be described as 'paschal'. Jesus is taken away from the disciples only for a short time, for the days of the Passion; then he returns and is permanently with them. The community lives in this awareness of the presence of Christ and, even though it suffers affliction in the world, it is still filled with the peace of Christ (16.33) and his imperishable joy.

Is this an unrealistic attitude, an attitude of estrangement from the world? We have an answer from the many young people who have followed the call to the 'council of youth' at Taizé. Young men and girls from all over the world, with very diverse experiences and expectations, yet all longing and seeking to cope with life together in a way better than formerly. A young French girl puts it this way: 'From Easter 1970, when the preparation for the council of youth was announced, a bridge was set up between the days spent at Taizé and ordinary life. Inwardly united with one another, often by small, provisional, and informal groups of young people, we are living out a spiritual adventure: the discovery of Christ, in himself, and of the joy which arises from him.'

These young people have also understood that the joy flowing from the presence of Christ raises a challenge: 'to commit one's life to securing that man is no longer the victim of man, so that all may share in the same joy of redemption'. They are critical of the traditional Christianity of the Churches. A young Italian said: 'The traditional forms of commitment in the Churches are no longer satisfying. We must find new, original forms corresponding to the conditions and needs of present-day life.' They must be oriented to the main themes of the gospel, 'the quest for God and for justice for man'. One of the girls engaged in the discussions observed: 'There are already such men and women. They are part of that movement which does not merely scratch at the surface.'

Are these not testimonies reflecting the style and aspiration of Johannine Christianity? And are they not hopeful signs of our time? So once again there arises the question of the signs of the time, which we have been trying to interpret. There are depressing and menacing phenomena which seem to point to storm and tempest, destruction and ruin. But there are other signs which are less glaring and yet visible and perceptible. There are salvific and vital forces which are effective in the depths of men's hearts, forces which work to bring together and unite the good, to liberate the oppressed, rescue the afflicted and needy, to establish reconciliation and peace. Essentially it is the one force of love which proceeds from God, has appeared in his Son Jesus Christ, and from then onwards never fades. It is continually touching and stirring people afresh, uniting them with each other and prompting them to deeds which raise up falling humanity, renew it and lead it into the future. This is the Advent hope with which we are continually filled. Wherever the history of mankind may lead, it will never again fall away from the love of God, who sent his Son into the world, not to judge the world, but so that the world might be saved by him (John 3.17).